# WINNING OVER WEIGHT

by
Marilyn Hickey

**HARRISON HOUSE**
Tulsa, Oklahoma

Unless otherwise indicated,
all Scripture quotations are taken from
the King James Version of the Bible.


13 12 11 10      46 45 44 43 42


Winning Over Weight
ISBN 13: 978-0-89274-248-6
ISBN 10: 0-89274-248-8
Copyright © 1982 by Marilyn Hickey
P.O. Box 17340
Denver, Colorado 80217


Published by Harrison House, Inc.
P. O. Box 35035
Tulsa, Oklahoma 74153

# Winning Over Weight

Always and forever, the Bible is practical. It's not just "pie in the sky," or fantasy, or something that collects dust on your coffee table. The Bible is a book you can live by! It works. It deals with where you live and is concerned with what concerns you! Therefore, the Bible is concerned with your eating habits. It has much to say that will help you in the area of your eating.

## The Trouble With Food

You are not the first person to have had trouble with food! What was the first thing Adam and Eve got into trouble over? Food! What did they eat? Forbidden fruit.

What did Esau get into trouble for? Eating beans. He loved lentils! It's not wrong to eat beans, but he sold his birthright for a bowl of beans. Food became his downfall!

Do you remember Belshazzar? The night Babylon fell he threw a big feast which turned into a drunken brawl. He drank from holy vessels. Food contributed to his fall from power.

There is another man in the Bible who literally fell because of overeating. He even passed on his bad eating habits to his sons. His name is Eli, and he was fatter than a forty-pound robin! He loved that fat meat! The Bible tells us this in 1 Samuel 1-4.

Eli's sons began to love fat too, and they would steal it from the sacrifices! God told Eli, "You get those sons under control or I'm going to take away your ministry." God warned Eli twice, but he liked to eat rather than obey!

Eli's situation is sad because he really did love God. But he could not give up his eating habits or discipline his sons. He was so over-weight that when he heard that the Ark of the Covenant had been stolen, he lost his balance and fell backwards off a stool, breaking his neck!

Wrong eating habits produce all kinds of bad things, but be encouraged, God has the way out of these bad habits!

# The Lusting For Food

All of us have a desire for food—that's only natural. Our bodies require food to sustain them. But when we get into the area of "lusting" after food, we're in trouble! When we talk about lusting, we usually think of it in the sexual realm. There is, however, an area of food lusts. If we can discover the cause for these, I think it will help you.

Once in a while I get a craving for a chocolate bar with almonds. It's not very often (thank goodness!), but when I do, I'm constantly thinking, "Chocolate with almonds. Chocolate with almonds!" One chocolate bar won't do much damage, but if I continue to eat chocolate bars with almonds, it could prove disastrous!

One time I tried to analyze when I especially found myself craving chocolate bars. I believe I found the answer to it in Proverbs, that good practical book on wisdom:

Slothfulness casteth into a deep sleep; and an idle soul shall suffer hunger (Prov.19:15).

Idle people are hungry people! Have you ever noticed that when you don't have much

3

to do and you don't have your mind on any-thing, that is the easiest time to run past the refrigerator and help yourself? Have you ever noticed that when you're not really busy, you tend to think more about food?

When we are not engaged in some mean-ingful activity, we can easily get hung up on food. It's good to keep busy. It will help you to become thin and stay thin.

It's good to keep your body busy, and it's good to keep your mind busy. Proverbs 27:7 says, The full soul loatheth an honeycomb; but to the hungry soul every bitter thing is sweet.

The soul is composed of the mind and the emotions. Notice that this verse speaks of a full soul: a mind that is full, complete; a mind that is constantly thinking about worthwhile things, worthwhile plans. People with full souls are not thinking about sweets all the time—they are too busy filling their minds with thoughts of achievement.

On the other hand, the hungry soul, or the person whose mind is idle and undisciplined, thinks that everything tastes good. Even bitter things taste good to this person! Keep your body busy, and keep your mind busy and full of the Word—that will cause your eating habits to be pleasing to the Lord.

Another key to eating properly is found in Proverbs 13:25:

The righteous eateth to the satisfying of his soul: but the belly of the wicked shall want.

The important word to see here is satisfying. You can eat to the satisfying of your soul or you can go beyond that amount and stuff yourself! Most of the time we go beyond being satisfied because the food tastes so good.

The righteous don't go beyond being satisfied; they stay within that limit.

We all like pastries, don't we? They are marvelous! One time my husband and I were in Finland to minister. I have never seen so many pastries in my life! Practically every other shop on every street had pastries in the windows. We thought we had to sample one of everything that was different. It got to be dangerous to go out of our hotel!

Scripture has some interesting things to say about pastries—it calls them "deceitful dainties." Proverbs 23:3 says, Be not desirous of his dainties: for they are deceitful meat. Overindulgence in sweets can hurt you. They look good, but looks can be deceiving!

Here is a verse that might surprise you: Proverbs 25:27, It is not good to eat much honey. That has to do with sweets. It is better to eat natural sweets like fruit. Honey is good, but too much of any good thing is dangerous—unless it is the Word!

We've covered the dangers in eating sweets; now let's look at the dangers in eating too much meat. I can remember several years ago when eating meat was supposed to pick you up if you were tired. There were bumper stickers which said, Eat beef; then the lamb people came out with something about eating lamb.

Soon scientists began to say that Americans had too much protein in their diets. Solomon knew thousands of years ago that consuming foods with too much protein was undesirable. He said in Proverbs 23:20, Be not among winebibbers; among riotous eaters of flesh. We area nation of meat eaters. Every restaurant serves meat—steak, steak, steak. Too much meat is not good, just like too many sweets is not good!

## The Eating of Food

Eating got Adam and Eve into trouble; it also got Esau, Eli and his sons, and Belshazzar into trouble. Eating sweets is not good, and eating too much meat is not good. None of us wants to overindulge and get into trouble with our eating. We want to be healthy people. The next question would naturally be, "What can I do to change my eating habits?"

The Bible tells us how to handle our craving for too much food. First, of course, it is good to confess the Word about your health. But I don't think it is good to confess the Word and then do everything wrong! Someone once told me he had so much faith that he threw his toothbrush away. That's not faith that's bad breath! The Bible gives us certain guidelines, and as much as we can, we need to obey those suggestions.

The first Scripture we need to consider in changing our eating habits is 1 Corinthians 10:31:

Whether therefore ye eat, or drink, or whatsoever ye do, do all to the glory of God.

Ask yourself if your eating habits glorify God. And remember, you can be skinny and still not glorify God in your eating! If, on the other hand, you look like a blimp, will people see God in you? If you have tried this and your body still doesn't seem to get in line, I will give you something a little stronger!

Proverbs 23:2 says, And put a knife to thy throat, if thou be a man given to appetite. That is pretty serious! Get strong with yourself and say, "I have taken this lust for food to the cross, and I reckon myself dead to this sin and alive unto God." Saying this is a little better than actually putting a knife to your throat, but the idea of putting a knife to our throats shows how serious we need to be when it comes to wrong eating habits.

Somebody always says, "But what if I starve to death?"

I have a good answer for that! Proverbs 10:3 says, The Lord will not suffer the soul of the righteous to famish: but he casteth away the substance of the wicked. God will not allow you to starve; don't let the devil feed you a lie.

When I am traveling, there is sometimes little opportunity to eat at a convenient time. I will hold a meeting, then have to catch an early plane to the next meeting. Normally I don't like to eat before a service because my mind doesn't have the recall it should. I am not as spiritually alive if I eat a big meal before a meeting.

I don't usually eat breakfast, so that by three or four o'clock I'm really hungry. That's when I eat a heavy meal. After the evening meetings I'm hungry again, but by then it's late and I don't want to eat right before going to bed. It's not good for your sleep or for your body!

But my mind will say, "You'll starve if you don't eat something now. You'll really get sick if you don't eat more food." Isn't that ridiculous! I wouldn't get sick on one good meal a day. I could make it very well. I have to cast down the lie of the enemy and discipline myself to stick to correct eating habits.

One of the best ways to handle a bad eating habit is to pray in the Spirit. Romans 8:26 says:

Likewise the Spirit also helpeth our infirmities: for we know not what we should pray for as we ought: but the Spirit itself maketh intercession for us with groanings which cannot be uttered.

What is an infirmity? It is a weakness. The Spirit helps you when you are not firm, when you are not strong or disciplined.

Are you firm in the area of proper eating? If not, pray in the Spirit before you sit down to eat. The Spirit will help you when you are weak. Pray for ten minutes before you begin to eat. Pray in the Spirit before you pass the refrigerator. Praying in the Spirit will help you in your area of weakness and turn it into one of your areas of strength.

We have looked at the dangers involved in eating, what not to eat, and some ways of breaking bad eating habits. Now, let's be positive and examine how to eat. Proverbs 18:20 says, A man's belly shall be satisfied with the fruit of his mouth; and with the increase of his lips shall he be filled.

Speak right things about your food before you eat it. Speak a positive word over your meals. It may not look like something from the Hilton, but it will taste a lot better if you speak well of it, rather than complaining about it.

When our children, Mike and Sarah, were growing up, if they said, "I don't like that!" my husband would say, "We like everything at this house; we like it all." Mike and Sarah would have to take a little of everything on their plate, whether they liked it or not. Guess what happened over a period of time? You're right! They began to like everything!

Mike told me one time that he was just amazed at how many kids his age were picky eaters. He said, "It's just disgusting that so many of my friends don't like this and don't like that. I like everything!"

I asked him, "What do you think made you like that?"

"Dad!" That was all he said.

Speak right things before you eat. If you make a face or say something bad about your food before you eat, you set up your body to reject what you are eating, and you will lose out on the nutrition your body needs.

Many people are in trouble over food because they eat when they are depressed. Proverbs has something to say about this too: All the days of the afflicted are evil: but he that is of a merry heart hath a continual feast (Prov. 15:15).

Eat when you are happy, and it will be a feast to you. It could be crackers and milk, but you'll be happy. It will taste good to you. Whatever you eat when you are happy will be a continual feast. You will receive more strength from your food if you eat it with joy. Nehemiah says this in chapter 8, verse 10:

. . . eat the fat, and drink the sweet, and send portions unto them for whom nothing is prepared . . . for the joy of the Lord is your strength.

If you are depressed, stay away from food! If your emotions are bad, your food will knot up in your stomach. The Bible puts it this way in Proverbs 15:17: Better is the dinner of herbs where love is, than a stalled ox and hatred therewith.

Don't eat when you are uptight. Eating at times like these can cause physical illness. How do you think people get ulcers? They get them by eating when they are nervous, when there is unforgiveness in their spirit, when they are full of hatred. Correct your attitude first, then eat with joy and you will have a continual feast.

The Bible goes on to tell us to eat with temperance:

Hast thou found honey? eat so much as is sufficient for thee, lest thou be filled therewith, and vomit it.

Proverbs 25:16

Isn't the Bible right on our level? Keep yourself in balance. Eat only what you know you can handle—only what is sufficient.

Do you like chocolate chip cookies? My, couldn't you just eat a dozen of them before you know it? That's oversufficiency! Your body knows what is sufficient. If you overdo it, this verse says that you will vomit. No one should come to that place!

Ask the Lord to help you in this area of temperance. Before you sit down to eat, tell yourself that you will eat only that which is sufficient for you.

One Scripture I have loved for years is Proverbs 30:8. I have taken it in a spiritual way and also in a natural way.

Remove far from me vanity and lies: give me neither poverty nor riches; feed me with food convenient for me.

We need to get our eyes off physical food and be fed with what is really necessary for our growth. We need to feed ourselves a balanced diet of physical and spiritual food.

Ask the Lord to give you what is convenient for you at this time. It may be that you need to be encouraged from the Word in a particular situation so that your eating habits get in line with the guidelines we have been studying.

## The Sanctifying of Food

One of the most important aspects of eating, and something that will help you to keep a right attitude in your eating, is found in 1 Timothy 4:3-5:

Forbidding to marry, and commanding to abstain from meats, which God hath created to be received with thanksgiving of them which believe and know the truth.

For every creature of God is good, and nothing to be refused, if it be received with thanksgiving: for it is sanctified by the word of God and prayer.

These verses tell us that we do not have to be vegetarians. Every creature is good for food. Remember, though, that we are not to be riotous eaters of flesh.

Did you know that what you pray over, giving thanks, is set apart by the Lord for your well-being? I believe that if nutrition is lacking in what you have to eat, God can make it up to you if you will give thanks for it and pray over it.

However, that doesn't mean you can neglect good meal planning. But sometimes you may be in a position where you can't eat correctly. I fly quite often, and I know that the food on planes isn't always the most nutritious. I like to claim Deuteronomy 7:13-15 over my food. It says that the Lord will bless my meat and drink and take away all sickness.

And he will love thee, and bless thee, and multiply thee: he will also bless the fruit of thy womb, and the fruit of thy land, thy corn, and thy wine, and thine oil, the increase of thy kine, and the flocks of thy sheep, in the land which he sware unto thy fathers to give thee.

Thou shalt be blessed above all people: there shall not be male or female barren among you, or among your cattle.

And the Lord will take away from thee all sickness, and will put none of the evil diseases of Egypt, which thou knowest, upon thee; but will lay them upon all them that hate thee.

If you believe everything you hear or read about food, you will become frustrated: "Bacon causes cancer," "Coffee causes cancer," etc. If you followed it all, you wouldn't know what to eat!

Ask God to bless and sanctify your food, and He will take away sickness from you. You can't always be extremely selective about what you eat, but you can pray the right thing over your food before you eat it.

I believe that sometimes God has protected our ministry team because of the right confessions of our mouths. Let me share one experience that occurred while we were in Mexico.

We went to a little village way out in the country. After church we were asked to stay and eat. The people were warm and friendly, and we couldn't refuse. To this day I am not sure what was in the meal we ate! It was a very poor town, and I didn't see many dogs around—seriously! Could the meat that was served have been dog?

The people said we were eating mole'. I've had mole' before—chicken and turkey—and I like it. But I thought at the time, If this is dog mole', I'm going to eat it and like it! Lord, I'm receiving this with thanksgiving and prayer. I ate it all and didn't get sick.

Some people go to Mexico and come home sick, but we didn't! I was speaking the right thing. That food was "set apart" for me through thanksgiving and prayer.

## The Choosing of Food

The Bible gives us an idea of what we should eat. When he (Paul) therefore was come up again, and had broken bread, and eaten, and talked a long while, even till break of day, so he departed.

Acts 20:11

Paul had a habit of eating bread with believers. They did it for fellowship. Something goes on in eating with others that brings a unity.

Paul ate with a great expectation: he expected to be healthy from his eating. He expected something out of the bread that many others didn't understand. A good example of this is seen in Acts 27. Paul warned the owners of a ship not to sail because of impending danger. They refused to listen to him and sailed anyway. A tremendous storm arose, and it looked like they were all going to die.

Paul fasted and prayed and urged the others to do the same. Surprisingly, the unsaved members of the crew of that ship fasted with Paul. After fourteen days Paul received a visit from an angel telling him that no one would die.

Wherefore, Paul said, I pray you to take some MEAT: for this is for your health (Acts

27:34). God is practical! He knew that those men needed some meat for their health.

And when he had thus spoken, he took BREAD, and gave thanks to God in presence of them all: and when he had broken it, he began to eat (v. 35). Then notice verse 36: Then were they all of good cheer, and they also took some meat.

Pay careful attention to what Paul ate and what the crew ate. They did not eat the same thing. The unsaved crew ate meat, while Paul ate bread. If meat was good for the crew, why wasn't it good for Paul? I believe the Lord has given me the correct answer.

When the early Christians met together, they often had a communion service. They broke bread and drank together as they celebrated the death and resurrection of Jesus. The bread they ate was leavened bread, which is most significant.

Throughout the Old Testament, in most instances, the bread that was used in the religious feasts was unleavened bread because leaven was a type of sin. But in 1 Corinthians 11:23,24 Paul says that Jesus took bread: and when he had given thanks, he brake it, and said, Take, eat.

The bread mentioned in the above Scripture is leavened bread, or raised bread. In Acts 27 it says that Paul ate raised bread (the Greek word artos used in both verses signifies a raised bread) and the crew ate meat.

Why did Paul eat raised bread in Acts 27, and why did the early Christians eat raised bread? Because the raised bread represented the raised body of Jesus! The raised bread symbolized resurrection power to them!

When we partake of communion, we should expect resurrection power to operate in our bodies. We should expect all sickness to be taken away from us! But we must eat the right kind of food! If you are tempted to eat a blueberry pie or a piece of cake, think of eating "raised bread." Think of partaking of resurrection power—the power you need to overcome all those bad eating habits. The more resurrection power you feed to your mind and body, the easier it will become to say, "No!" to bad eating habits.

# The Kingdom of Food

By way of review, the following points have been covered to help you maintain a proper diet and stay in shape physically, so that your body will look the way God intends for it to. We have looked at all the troubles food can bring to people and have seen how to deal with food lusts, how to eat different kinds of food, how to "set apart" our food and have it produce strength and good health in our bodies. Last of all, we have learned to choose the most important food of all—the "raised bread" that brings resurrection power into our eating habits.

The last point is without doubt the most important one. Paul said in Romans 14:17:

For the kingdom of God is not meat and drink: but righteousness, and peace, and joy in the Holy Ghost.

We are not to major on the "kingdom of food," but we are to major on the Kingdom of God.

Do not dwell on your eating habits, whether you are too fat or too skinny. Today, take your eyes off the problem and put your eyes on the

Kingdom of God. Pray in the Spirit and begin to devour the "raised bread" that will supply all the power you need to overcome bad eating habits.

Here are some practical steps to change your eating habits and see your figure improve:

1. Keep your mind active—think on right things. (Prov. 19:15; 27:7.)

2. Don't eat to stuff yourself, but to satisfy yourself. (Prov. 13:25.)

3. Watch your intake of sweets and meats. (Prov. 23:3,20.)

4. When you eat, do it to glorify God. (1 Cor. 10:31.)

5. Take your bad eating habits to the cross and reckon them dead. (Prov. 23:2.)

6. Pray in the Spirit for ten minutes before you sit down to eat. (Rom. 8:26,27.)

7. Speak right words about your food before you eat. (Prov. 18:20.)

8. Don't eat when you are depressed. (Prov. 15:15.)

9. Pray God's Word over your food. (1 Tim. 4:4,5; Deut. 7:13-15.)

Now that you have finished this practical little booklet, act on God's Word. It will work for you and help you win over weight!

# Prayer of Salvation

God loves you—no matter who you are, no matter what your past. God loves you so much that He gave His one and only begotten Son for you. The Bible tells us that "…whoever believes in him shall not perish but have eternal life" (John 3:16 NIV). Jesus laid down His life and rose again so that we could spend eternity with Him in heaven and experience His absolute best on earth. If you would like to receive Jesus into your life, say the following prayer out loud and mean it from your heart.

*Heavenly Father, I come to You admitting that I am a sinner. Right now, I choose to turn away from sin, and I ask You to cleanse me of all unrighteousness. I believe that Your Son, Jesus, died on the cross to take away my sins. I also believe that He rose again from the dead so that I might be forgiven of my sins and made righteous through faith in Him. I call upon the name of Jesus Christ to be the Savior and Lord of my life. Jesus, I choose to follow You and ask that You fill me with the power of the*

*Holy Spirit. I declare that right now I am a child of God. I am free from sin and full of the righteousness of God. I am saved in Jesus' name. Amen.*

If you prayed this prayer to receive Jesus Christ as your Savior for the first time, please contact us on the web at **www.harrisonhouse.com** to receive a free book.

Or you may write to us at
**Harrison House**
P.O. Box 35035
Tulsa, Oklahoma 74153

# Fast. Easy.
# Convenient.

**harrison**house.com

For the latest Harrison House product information and author news, look no further than your computer. All the details on our powerful, life-changing products are just a click away. New releases, E-mail subscriptions, Podcasts, testimonies, monthly specials—find it all in one place. Visit harrisonhouse.com today!

**harrison**house

# *Covering the Earth with His Word!*

Ministering to both physical as well as spiritual needs is at the heart of Marilyn Hickey Ministries and Marilyn's call to "cover the earth with the Word" in the uttermost parts of the world in places such as . . .

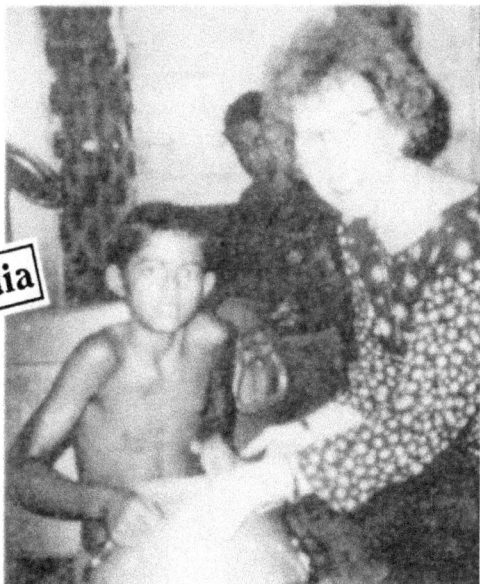

India

Pakistan

China

Hungary

# God's Covenant For Your Family

by Marilyn Hickey

God has good things for you and your family. They are all part of His covenant with you as His child. When you enter into God's new covenant, many promises become yours— promises not only for you, but also for your mate and for your children.

God is concerned about your total existence—spiritual, emotional, and physical. He wants all of your life to be fulfilling and delightful.

Marilyn Hickey

Books by Marilyn Hickey

...He Will Give You Another Helper

Breaking Generational Curses

Winning Over Weight

Women of the Word

God's Benefit: Healing

Available at your local Christian bookstore.

Harrison House
Tulsa, OK 74153

www.ingramcontent.com/pod-product-compliance
Lightning Source LLC
Chambersburg PA
CBHW060552030426
42337CB00019B/3520